A Kid's Guide to Drawing™

How to Draw Cartoon Vehicles

Curt Visca and Kelley Visca

The Rosen Publishing Group's
PowerKids Press™
New York

Dedicated to Curt's parents, Norman and Ellen, who have "steered him in the right direction" and encouraged him to pursue his cartooning talents

Published in 2004 by The Rosen Publishing Group, Inc.
29 East 21st Street, New York, NY 10010

First Edition

Editor: Natashya Wilson
Book Design: Kim Sonsky
Layout Design: Michael J. Caroleo

Illustration Credits: All illustrations © Curt Visca.
Photo Credits: Cover and p. 14 © Carl & Ann Purcell/CORBIS; p. 6 © Reuters NewMedia Inc./CORBIS; p. 8 © Kevin R. Morris/CORBIS; p. 10 © Jonathan Blair/CORBIS; p. 12 George Hall/CORBIS; p. 16 © James Kay/Index Stock; p. 18 © Bettmann/CORBIS; p. 20 © Tria Giovan/CORBIS.

Visca, Curt.
How to draw cartoon vehicles / Curt Visca and Kelley Visca.— 1st ed.
    p. cm. — (A kid's guide to drawing)
Summary: Provides facts about different kinds of vehicles and step-by-step instructions for drawing cartoons of each one, including a submarine, a hot-air balloon, and a racecar.
Includes bibliographical references and index.
ISBN 0-8239-6724-7 (lib. bdg.)
1. Vehicles in art—Juvenile literature. 2. Cartooning—Technique—Juvenile literature. [1. Vehicles in art. 2. Cartooning—Technique. 3. Drawing—Technique.] I. Visca, Kelley. II. Title. III. Series.
NC825.V45 V57 2004
741.5—dc21
                                        2002008656

Manufactured in the United States of America

CONTENTS

Cartoon Vehicles

A vehicle **transports**, or carries, people and things from one place to another. One of the first vehicles used long ago was called a sledge. It was made from a forked tree branch and worked like a sled. Once the wheel was invented in about 3000 B.C., two-wheeled carts became the first road vehicles.

You probably travel in one or more vehicles every day. Unless you walk to school, you probably ride in a school bus, in a car, on a bicycle, or on a scooter. These are four different types of vehicles.

The eight vehicles that you will learn about in this book can transport you over land, through the air, and in the water. You will learn many facts about these vehicles and how to draw a cartoon of each one.

Cartoon drawings are different from **realistic** drawings. Real vehicles don't have eyes, noses, and mouths, but these cartoon vehicles do! When you draw, you will include only the most important lines and shapes, keeping your drawings simple. You may find that your vehicles look different from the ones in the book. That's OK! As a cartoonist, you will develop your own cartooning style, or way of drawing. This **unique** style will set your drawings apart and give your cartoons their own personality. To make your vehicles funnier, you may choose to draw some parts differently. For example, you may make larger eyes or larger noses. Be creative!

You will need the following supplies to draw cartoon vehicles:

- Paper
- A sharp pencil or a felt-tipped marker
- An eraser
- Colored pencils or crayons to add color

Draw your cartoons at a desk, a table, or another quiet place with a lot of light and all your supplies nearby. The directions under each drawing step will help you to add new parts to your cartoon. The new parts are shown in red. The drawing shapes and terms are described and defined in the Terms for Drawing Cartoons list on page 22. Remember to work slowly, do your best, and practice your cartoons. Now zip on over to the next page and get carried away by cartoon vehicles!

The Submarine

The submarine is a torpedo-shaped ship built to travel under  water. Most submarines are used by the military, but some are used for scientific study. Dutch inventor Cornelis Drebbel made the first submarine in 1620. He covered a wooden rowboat with leather to make it watertight. It was powered by oars. Today most submarines are made of metal and are powered by **nuclear energy**. They range from 290 to 560 feet (88–171 m) in length and carry from 130 to 160 crew members. When a submarine is underwater, crew members use the **periscope** to see above the surface. They talk with people on land by radio. The antennae on top of the submarine send and receive the radio messages. There are also windows called portholes on the sides of a submarine. Submarines can travel through the water unnoticed. A submarine can dive underwater in less than 1 minute. They can dive to depths of about 1,500 feet (457 m).

1

Draw a circle and a curved line for the eyes.
Add a dot in each eye. Draw a letter C for
the nose, then add a short straight line.
Make a thick curved line for the mouth.

2

Make a short line behind the eyes. Add two
bent lines with a letter C on top for the
periscope. Shade in an oval inside the C.
Make two rectangles with thin triangles on top
for antennae. Draw lines to finish the top.

3

You did it! Next start under the mouth and
draw a flattened circle for the body. Make the
right side pointy.

4

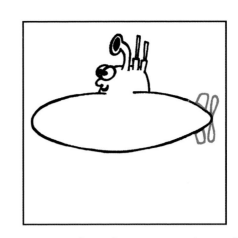

At the pointy end, make two teardrops for
the propeller, the part that moves the
submarine. Draw curved lines in front of the
propeller for the rudder. It steers the sub.

5

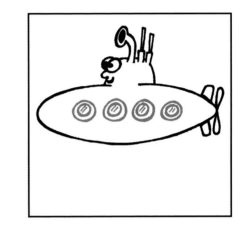

Beautiful! Make four circles for the portholes.
Add a smaller circle inside each porthole.
Put angled lines in the portholes for detail.

6

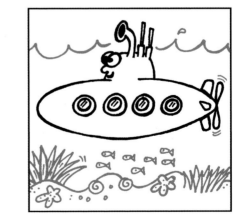

Draw action lines to show
movement. Create your
own ocean bottom, sea
creatures, and water.

The Hot-Air Balloon

In France in 1783, a sheep, a duck, and a rooster became the first **passengers** to float in a hot-air balloon. In 1793, George Washington saw the start of the first manned balloon flight in the United States. The balloon floated from Philadelphia to New Jersey. In March 1999, Bertrand

Piccard of Switzerland and Brian Jones of Great Britain became the first balloonists to fly around the world nonstop. The 25,402-mile (40,881-km) trip lasted for 19 days, 21 hours, and 55 minutes.

The bag, or balloon-shaped part, of today's hot-air balloons is made of a special, strong fabric. It has a large opening, called the mouth, at the bottom. Heat made by a gas burner rises through the mouth into the bag. Because hot air rises above cooler air, the hot-air-filled bag lifts the attached basket into the air.

1

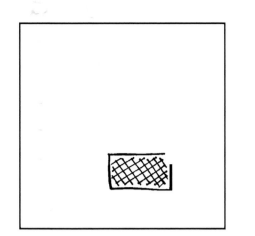

Start with the balloon's basket by making a rectangle with an open upper-right corner. Inside add angled lines in both directions.

2

Draw the duck's eyes. Add eyebrows. Make a letter *S* for the beak, and add a curved line under it. Draw a curved line for the head and two lines for the neck. Draw curved lines to make the back and the tail feathers.

3

For the rooster, use circles and dots for the eyes, zigzag lines for a beak, and curved lines for the head and body. Draw the sheep's face. Make wiggly lines for its body. Add hooves.

4

Nice work on this detailed drawing! For the burner, draw a square above the rooster's head, and add a rectangle on top. Add two bent lines on either side of the square.

5

Above the burner, make a flattened circle. Draw a straight line and a curved line on each side to show the bottom of the balloon's bag. Add straight lines on both sides to connect the bag to the basket.

6

Add detail. Make action lines. Draw another hot-air balloon on the left side. Add clouds. Well done!

9

The School Bus

Each year in the United States, 24 million children ride 450,000 public school buses more than 4 billion miles (6 billion km) to and from school! New York City public schools have the largest number of daily riders. They transport about 186,350 students on 5,500 buses each day.

Public transportation to schools began in the late 1800s. The first vehicles to take students to and from schools were horse-drawn carts borrowed from local farmers. In 1915, the first school bus was made in South Dakota. It was called the Model F. In 1939, "school bus yellow" became the official color for school buses. Today school buses have warning lights and a stop sign that swings out from the bus's side to tell cars that children are getting on or off the bus.

1

Let's begin by making an oval with a letter C on its left side for eyes. Add a smaller oval in each eye, and shade it in. Draw a slightly bent line for the front of the bus.

2

Draw a short line behind the eyes. Make a long curved line for the top and back of the bus. Add a square for the bumper and a vertical line under it.

3

Super effort! Make ovals for the front and back wheels. Add a smaller oval inside each wheel for hubcaps. Draw three horizontal lines for the bottom of the bus.

4

Wow! Draw a small letter C for the nose. Make a horizontal line and a letter U for the mouth. Add two vertical lines and one horizontal line for teeth.

5

Draw two curved lines under the bus for the second front and back wheels. Make triangles with one curved side for the front and back windows. Draw rectangles for the four middle windows. You're almost there!

6

Finish your drawing by adding detail. Write "SCHOOL BUS." Add a caption. Ride safely!

The Jet

Brothers Orville and Wilbur Wright made history when they built and flew the first manned flying machine, the *Flyer*, near Kitty Hawk,  North Carolina. Their first flight, on December 17, 1903, lasted for 12 seconds and traveled a distance of 120 feet (36.5 m). The airplanes and jets built and flown today provide a faster way to transport passengers and **cargo**. They can travel between 500 and 600 miles per hour (805–966 km/h) and can cross the United States in fewer than 5 hours. A jet can fly because its rounded, angled wings create **lift**. The wings' shape causes the air flowing under the wings to press on them more than the air flowing over the wings. The higher pressure underneath causes the plane to rise. Jet planes have many uses. They carry passengers to faraway places and are used to fight forest fires, deliver mail and packages, and fight wars.

1

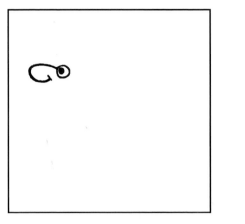

Let's give our jet a face by drawing a circle and a dot for the eye. Make a letter *C* and a short straight line for the front of the jet and the mouth.

2

Terrific! Make a slightly curved line for the bottom of the jet. Draw a curved line for the nose and shade it in. Add a curved line and a dot for the other eye.

3

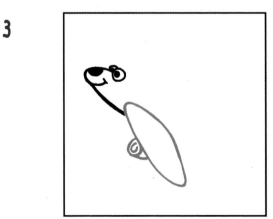

Draw a triangle shape with rounded corners to make the wing. Make an engine using three curved lines.

4

Draw two curved lines for the top and bottom of the jet. Add an upside-down letter *U* and a small triangle for the tail fins.

5

Fantastic! Make two upside-down letter *U*'s for the other wing and tail fin. Draw curved lines to make the other engine.

6

Add circles for windows, rectangle shapes for flaps on the wings and tail, and action lines. Draw curved lines for clouds. Good work!

13

The Boat

Boats are used to transport people across lakes, oceans, and other bodies of water. There are many different kinds of boats. Early boats and canoes were made of hollowed-out logs. Today boats range from

small rowboats that can seat only a few people to cruise ships and aircraft carriers that can carry thousands of people. Sailboats are powered by the wind and are named for the ways in which their sails and **masts** are **rigged**. A sloop has two sails and one mast. **Ketches**, **schooners**, and **yawls** have two masts and at least three sails. The motorboat is another type of boat. The most popular motorboats are those with outboard motors, or motors outside the **hull** of the boat. Tugboats range in length from 70 to 210 feet (21–64 m). These strong, wooden boats with rubber tires or cushions on their sides are used to guide and tow different types of ships into and out of port.

1

Let's draw a tugboat! Start by making a circle and a letter *C* for the eyes. Add two dots for pupils. Draw a horizontal line on top and two vertical lines down the sides.

2

Wonderful job! Draw a small letter *C* for the nose. Make a small horizontal line and a small letter *U* for the mouth. Shade it in.

3

Ahoy! Draw a horizontal line and two short vertical lines for the cabin. Draw three circles with smaller circles inside for portholes.

4

You did it! Draw three more circles with smaller circles inside for bumpers. Make eight horizontal lines to connect the bumpers. Add vertical lines on the ends.

5

Make a large letter *U* for the hull. Draw a backward letter *C* and two teardrops for the propeller. Land ho!

6

Draw curved lines for smoke and water. Make eyebrows. Add action lines and detail.

The Helicopter

A helicopter flies by using two powerful **propellers** called rotors. It can fly up, down, forward, or backward. It can also **hover**, or stay in one spot in the air. The first model helicopter that

could fly was built by Frenchmen Launoy and Bienvenu in 1784. The first manned helicopter was flown in 1907. Built by Frenchman Louis Breguet, the helicopter lifted one of Breguet's assistants 2 feet (61 cm) into the air for 1 minute. Helicopters can take off and land in small areas. They can fly for as long as 2 to 3 hours for distances of nearly 600 miles (966 km) before they need more gas. Using helicopters for **rescues** has saved more than three million lives. Firefighters use them to drop water on fires. Police officers use them to look for lost people and escaped prisoners. Television and radio stations use helicopters while covering news stories.

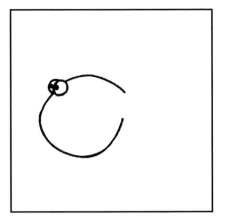

Draw a circle and a letter C for the eyes. Add a big dot inside each eye. Make a slightly curved line on the top and a curved line below the eyes for the cabin.

2

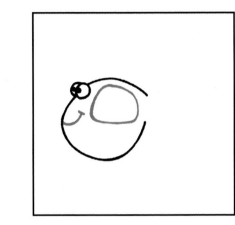

Outstanding work! Make a rounded shape for the window. Draw a curved line with a short line at the end for the mouth.

3

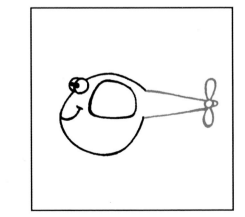

I'm proud of you! Draw two angled lines for the tail of the helicopter. Make a small circle, two teardrops, and a small, backward letter C for the tail rotor.

4

For the main rotor, make a flattened circle over the eyes. Draw a curved line and a short line to connect it to the top. Add another flattened circle to finish the rotor.

5

To make the front runner, draw four vertical lines. Make a bent line on the left and two horizontal lines. Finish it with a long bent line and a vertical line. Add the back runner.

6

Make mountains and a cloud using curved lines. Draw action lines. Add detail. I'm impressed!

The Racecar

Racecars travel at an average speed of 200 miles per hour (322 km/h). They race around oval tracks or on road-racing courses. Car racing is one of

the most popular **spectator** sports in the world. Each year more than 500,000 people watch the Indianapolis 500 race. It is the nation's largest paid-admission sporting event. Formula One and NASCAR are two other types of car racing. Formula One racecars are the most expensive cars to build. NASCAR, or stock-car racing, is the most popular type of racing. NASCAR cars have to be American made. They are raced on **superspeedways** that have wide turns with high **banks**.

Car racing is dangerous. Drivers wear safety helmets and **flame-resistant** clothing for protection. They always wear their seat belts!

1

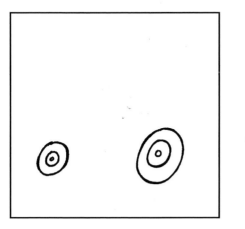

Let's draw an Indianapolis 500 racecar! Make three circles on the left for the front tire and three bigger circles on the right for the back tire.

2

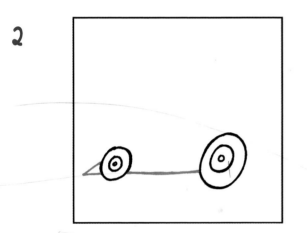

Draw a sideways letter V for the front of the racecar. Add a horizontal line for the bottom.

3

Nice work! From behind the front wheel, draw an angled line, then three straight lines up, over, and down. Add a bent line for the driver's area. You're halfway done!

4

Make a short line, a letter V, and a bent line. Draw the spoiler, the part that sticks up on top, using straight lines. Add another bent line, then use straight lines to finish the back.

5

Start your driver with two letter U's and two straight lines for goggles. Make curved lines for the nose, jaw, and helmet. Draw a mouth. Add curved and straight lines for the arms, hand, body, and steering wheel.

6

Add detail, action lines, smoke, and dust to your car. Give it a number. Make a railing and fans.

The Motorcycle

In 1885, Gottlieb Daimler of Germany built the first motorcycle by attaching an engine and two training wheels to his bicycle. In 1903, American inventor William Harley, his neighbor Arthur Davidson, and Davidson's brothers built the first Harley-Davidson motorcycle. Harley-Davidsons are still popular today.

Many people enjoy riding motorcycles as touring bikes on long trips. Other people use them for transportation to and from their job because motorcycles cost less to drive than do cars. Some riders race motorcycles on dirt courses with jumps, hills, and sharp turns in contests called **motocrosses**. Police officers also ride motorcycles. They are easy to move through traffic if the officer has to chase a speeding car and **enforce** traffic laws.

20

1

Make a circle and a letter C for the eyes. Add dots. Draw a rectangle around the eyes and a thin rectangle at the bottom. Make a letter C for the nose. Add the mouth.

2

Make each handlebar using two bent lines and a short vertical line. Add a thick straight line for hand grips. Make a bent line under the front grip for a gearshift. Draw a bent line and a square for the rearview mirror.

3

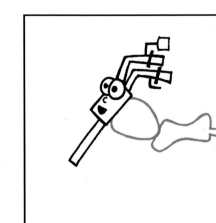

Next make an egg-shaped curved line for the gas tank. Make a wavy, squeeze-bottle shape for the seat using curved and straight lines. Sensational work!

4

Draw two bent lines under the gas tank. Connect their right ends. Draw two curvy letter V's for the front fender. Add a line and a bump on top. Make a bent line under the seat.

5

You're a great artist! Draw three long curved lines for the front tire. Make a small circle in the middle. Add eight straight lines for wheel spokes. Use curved and straight lines to make the back tire.

6

Make up a caption bubble. Add zigzag lines on the tires. Draw more lines for detail. Excellent!

21

Terms for Drawing Cartoons

Here are some of the words and shapes that you will use to draw cartoon vehicles:

𝆑	Action lines	S	Letter S	
⫽	Angled lines	U	Letter U	
⌐⌐	Bent lines	V	Letter V	
⌒	Caption	O	Oval	
O	Circle	▭	Rectangle	
⌒	Curved line	☐	Square	
Ɛ∵ᵘᵘ	Detail	≡	Straight lines	
∴∙	Dots	◯	Teardrop	
⬭	Flattened circle	▬	Thick line	
—	Horizontal line	△	Triangle	
C	Letter C			Vertical line
		⋜	Zigzag lines	

Glossary

banks (BANKS) Slopes in a road that make one side higher than the other.

cargo (KAR-goh) The load of goods carried by an airplane, a ship, or a truck.

enforce (en-FORS) To put or keep in force.

flame-resistant (FLAYM-rih-zis-tent) Made not to burn.

hover (HUH-ver) To fly in place in the air.

hull (HUL) The frame, or body, of a ship.

ketches (KECH-ez) Sailboats with two masts and with its sails set lengthwise. The rear mast is farther forward than the rear mast on a yawl.

lift (LIFT) The force of air on a plane's wings that makes the plane fly.

masts (MASTS) Long poles that rise from the deck of a ship and hold the ship's sails and ropes.

motocrosses (MOH-toh-kros-ez) Races for motorcycles or bicycles on dirt courses that have sharp turns and hills.

nuclear energy (NOO-klee-ur EH-nur-jee) The energy that exists in the nucleus, or center, of an atom, which is the smallest bit of matter.

passengers (PA-sin-jurz) People who ride in or on a moving thing.

periscope (PER-ih-skohp) A tool that is used to see above the surface of the water from below the surface.

propellers (pruh-PEL-erz) Paddlelike parts on a vehicle that spin to move the vehicle.

realistic (ree-uh-LIS-tik) Made to look real or true to life.

rescues (RES-kyooz) Acts of saving someone or something from danger.

rigged (RIGD) Supported by ropes and chains.

schooners (SKOO-nerz) Fast, sturdy boats with two masts.

spectator (SPEK-tay-ter) A person who sees or watches something without taking an active part.

superspeedways (SOO-per-speed-wayz) Racetracks with slanted turns that allow cars to make the turns at very high speeds.

transports (TRANZ-ports) Moves something from one place to another.

unique (yoo-NEEK) One of a kind.

yawls (YAHLZ) Sailboats with two masts. The rear mast is farther back than the rear mast on a ketch.

Index

Web Sites

Due to the changing nature of Internet links, PowerKids Press has developed an online list of Web sites related to the subject of this book. This site is updated regularly. Please use this link to access the list: www.powerkidslinks.com/kgd/vehicles/